# THREE SERMONS

## PATRICK HENRY GREENLEAF

HISTORICAL SERMONS

These texts were originally published in the United States.
The text is in the public domain.
Modern Edition © 2024
Historical Sermons

The publishers have made all reasonable efforts to ensure this book is indeed in the Public Domain in any and all territories it has been published.

**Sunday, a Christian Festival.** A Sermon Delivered in St. Paul's Church, November 14, 1858. By Patrick Henry Greenleaf, Rector of St .Paul's Church.

**The Office of Music in the Church of God**. A Sermon Delivered in St. Paul's Church, Cincinnati, on the Fifth Sunday after Trinity, 1856. By P.H. Greenleaf, D.D., Rector of the Church.

**The Substance of a Sermon,** Delivered in Saint John's Church, Charlestown, (Mass.), February 19, 1843. By Patrick Henry Greenleaf (1807-1869), Rector of the Church (1841-1851).

# CONTENTS

PART I
**SUNDAY, A CHRISTIAN FESTIVAL.**
Sermon                                    3

PART II
**THE OFFICE OF MUSIC IN THE CHURCH OF GOD.**
Sermon                                   17

PART III
**THE SUBSTANCE OF A SERMON**
Sermon                                   33
Alexander Viets Griswold                 43

*About the Author*                       47

# PART I

# SUNDAY, A CHRISTIAN FESTIVAL.

## A SERMON DELIVERED IN ST. PAUL'S CHURCH, NOVEMBER 14, 1858.

The following Sermon, prepared in the ordinary course of duty, with no reference to its publication, is now printed for the use of the Congregation, to correct some misrepresentations. A few notes have been added, more fully to explain the meaning of its text. And the Author sends it forth, with all its imperfections, desiring for himself and the cause he represents, "the truth, the whole truth, and nothing but the truth."

# SERMON

"And he said unto them, The Sabbath was made for man, and not man for the Sabbath; therefore the Son of Man is Lord also of the Sabbath."

— MARK 2:27, 28.

Our subject this morning is the Law of the Christian Sabbath. Its obligation rests not upon Jewish appointment. Its duties are not to be regulated by Jewish example.[1] It is a Christian day, founded upon the authority of Christ, celebrating the Resurrection of Christ, and is a Holy Day to be kept sacred in all its hours. It is a festival and not a fast—the feast of the resurrection of Jesus, and not a commemoration of Jewish history—a day consecrated by its duties—to holiness and therefore to happiness; and the rule of its observance is expressed by its Lord, in the words we have selected as our text, "The Sabbath was made for man, and not man for the Sabbath."

The true sanctification of the Lord's day, is in nowise promoted by severity and stringency in the mode of its observance. In the delicate relations of the affections and interior emotions of the soul, specially in matters of religion, it is unsafe to legislate. Indeed, it seems to me that much of the desecration of the day—much of the laxity and carelessness—nay, infidelity of men in its personal obedience, can be traced to the overstraining of its prescribed duties, the Puritanic and legal severity of its law, and the mistaken view of its true nature and character, derived from considering it as a Jewish rather than a Christian institution; and on this subject, and with a view to correct some misapprehensions, I desire to say a few words.

At the time when the Lord spake the words of the text, He was in the fields of Judea. This divine man in no other temple than they afforded him, with no other dome above him than the sky, and no music around him but the songs of the birds and the whispering sighs of the trees, was fulfilling his great mission, and "about His Father's business." It was the Sabbath. Wherever else he had worshiped he was then in the temple of nature. His morning sacrifice had not been neglected. But his first duty to His Father having been performed, he was now in the open air and the green fields, walking with His Disciples. In their hunger they gathered the grains of corn as they passed, and did eat. The observant Pharisees complained of this, as a violation of the law forbidding "servile work," and held it to be a species of reaping. Our Lord repelled the idea of elevating an institution for man's benefit and comfort, above considerations of both; and referred to the case of David, who, in his necessities, did not scruple to take the consecrated Bread of the Sanctuary, as rightfully employed, if need be, in the sustenance of life. And then, calling their attention to the institution itself, as only means to an end, he rebuked their Pharisaic interpretation of the sacred Canon, by declaring that "the Sabbath was made for man," for his benefit, for his interests, for his comfort, for the higher necessities of his spiritual nature, and not to bind the man to the iron rule of any exterior law whatsoever. He intimates very broadly that no positive institution of the law was valuable unless it subserved the object for which it was given, and that in the new dispensation which he came to enact, He, in his official capacity as "the Son of Man," the Sent from God, was Lord of the time and the mode and the circumstances of the day—a power he soon after exercised in the change of the time to the first day of the week. And it is mainly on this authority of Christ to appoint institutions, and change times and seasons, that we rest the obligation of "the Sunday" as the Christian "Sabbath."

I consider the public worship of God, and open acknowledgement of his authority to be a moral duty; one which should regulate the moral conduct of intelligent creatures, and should bind a man's will and conscience; one which is acknowledged by reasonable men the moment it is stated. I regard the appointment of a time in which such duty might be executed, and by which its interests might be promoted, in the light of a positive precept; one requiring a duty of me, which was not before a duty; fixing a time for the execution of a duty which, at some other time, but for its law, I might have performed. I separate entirely the duty itself from the rule of its observance, And I consider that the law, which was addressed to man in the beginning, requiring the consecration of a seventh of time to religious purposes, and commanding a resting day in reference to the resting of God from his creative work, was addressed to man as a moral being, concerning a moral duty, and in no wise necessarily controlled by any direction as to the time or the manner of its observance. It was called "the rest of the Holy Sabbath,"[2] before the giving of the law of the ten commandments from Mount Sinai. And by whatever names and times it has since been known, it is addressed, not to a man's "rest," as a mere vacation of time, but it concerns his moral duties. And hence, in the fact of a conceded and agreed time, set apart by Apostolic usages,[3] by universal consent and the law of the Church of God,[4] for religious purposes, I see a decree of the Lord of the Sabbath as to the time and manner of my obedience.

You will perceive then, that I base the obligation of the observance of Sunday as holy time, upon its fact, as enacted by Church law, that it binds me—because in the Church Calendar are placed as festivals, "all Sundays in the year." But it is because of the authority of its moral duty, that I recognize its likeness in the moral code of the Ten Commandments; and only on that ground can its law have place there as binding at this day, and so still to be read in all our Churches for Christian learning. Otherwise the Sabbath of the Ten Commandments is only a Jewish law—a mere police regulation of ancient times.[5] When then I find in the Christian Dispensation the mediator Moses changed for the mediator Christ; the Aaronic Priesthood for the Christian Ministry; the Levitical Law for the Christian Gospel; and the Sacraments of the Circumcision and Passover for those of Baptism and the Supper of the Lord; I am prepared to find the Judaic Sabbath[6] exchanged for the Christian Feast of the Resurrection—a dark and gloomy solemnity giving place to a gladsome and beneficent festival, and the cry of death to the Sabbath breaker, fading away before the prayers of children, taught to say "Our Father," and to sing glad Hosannas to the Prince of Peace. And therefore, on a day sanctified by the Lord's personal presence, and the gift of his Holy Spirit[7] and called by divine inspiration the "Lord's Day," I yield to its obedience, as to a Law, prescribing a mode in which the highest moral duties may be executed and promoted, and by which society may be blest with the "Resting Day," commanded of God in the beginning.[8]

Leaving here, then the law of its authority, I pass to the mode and manner of its observance. As a festival, it is jubilant;[9] as the Lords' Day, it is holy; as as a sacred rest from ordinary and usual employments, it is separated forever from common uses; and its law to-day may well begin as did its enactment at Mt. Sinai, with an appeal to the memory of its sanctity in all time past. "Remember the Sabbath day to keep it Holy." But the application of its rule depends upon the social needs and the individual requirement. Special legislation on the subject, like sumptuary laws, tends to defeat the very purpose of the enactment, To provide by solemn statute "what a man shall eat, or what he shall drink, or wherewithal he shall be clothed," would be mischievous to the great interests of Temperance and Economy and Prudence, as if it were a premium offered for their disobedience. You can not legislate men into the Kingdom of Heaven, nor effect spiritual changes by legal enactments. You may lay down a broad rule for moral duty—you may appoint time and place for its obedience; but there it is wise to stop; and leave the relations of the soul in its duties to God to the individual conscience. Such is the prevailing impatience of control in matters of a religious and moral nature in this country, as that it is practically dangerous to legislate upon them farther than social necessities require. And in regard to the law of the Sunday, as it stands on the Statute Book of Ohio, our Supreme Court expressly declares that the principles of its foundation are wholly secular that it prescribes a day of rest from motives "of public policy;" that its provisions are "equally constitutional and obligatory, if some other day than Sunday had been named:" and that "the Statute derives no force whatever, from the fact that the Day of Rest it prescribes is Sunday."[10] So that all legislation in the matter is to be regarded as Police Regulation—as prohibitory of personal right, and therefore to be construed strictly; and that in a Court of Conscience the end to be attained, rises above all means prescribed, in value; and that all Church or State law on Sunday observance is to be construed in the light of that Higher law of its Lord—that "the Sabbath was made for man and not man for the Sabbath." The municipal law, contemplating a social need, and the Church law, contemplating a moral duty, happen to meet upon the same day, and the question before us as to the duties of the day, relates to both laws as here concurring.

Considering, then, the Lord of the Sabbath, as having both objects in view, it will help us to understand his meaning if we contrast for a moment Jewish severity and Christian liberty. By the Jewish law, the duties of the day were two fold—Negative and Positive. Negative—"That no man go out of his place:"[11] and "whosoever doeth work therein shall be put to death."[12] Positive—By sacrifice to God, public prayer, reading and hearing Holy Scripture; and by tradition that no man in a place of worship on that day should "sit down," however weary, or "carry a staff" however feeble, or do other than "stand in a posture of attention, one foot even with another." And the Rabbinical Rule was, that "nothing of labor which could possibly be done the day before, or put off to the day after, was lawful."

Jesus relaxed the severity of Jewish rule. "My Father worketh hitherto (on the Sabbath,) and I also work."[13] "He daily openeth his hand and filleth all things living with plenteousness."[14] And, says an Apostle, "Let no man judge you in respect to the Sabbath day,"[15] referring to the repeal of the Jewish law by the Christian Dispensation. It is remarkable that the greater part of all the recorded works of charity and mercy performed by our Lord, were done on the Sabbath day. We find him walking in the fields, as if to indicate the abrogation of the law, that "no man go out of his place:" commanding the comfort, the convenience, the happiness, even, of the ox and the ass, instead of the Rabbinical rule of absolute rest: and teaching by powerful example, that the benefit, the blessing, the truest interests of the body and the soul of man, were superior to all local regulations, and were the great ends by which all rules on the subject were to be marshaled. His words to the Pharisees, who would forbid the hungry to eat on that day, declare that its Law must be interpreted by the needs, moral and social, of the man for whom it was instituted. And our own civil Judiciary have only followed his steps by declaring that the "works of necessity," which form the statutory exception to the law of "no work," are not only those which are uncontrollable, but "those created by the exigencies of society or trade." Those "needs" may sometimes require him (they tell us) to go into the field to reap his wheat on the Sunday, or into the mill to grind his corn.[16] And surely nothing of labor which promotes the worship of God; which facilitates its extension; which aids the purpose of the Christian Assembly, or the grand end and design of the day, should be supposed to come within a prohibition which classes the forbidden labor with "rioting, quarreling and intemperance." Whether it be the labor which draws the carriage to church, or that which feeds the hungry in the family; whether it be the poor man's omnibus, or the rich man's coach. that is concerned —we will abide the judgment of the law, if they come not within the exceptions of the statute. And I can not but regard any attempt to discriminate in the modes of public conveyance to Church on the Lord's day, as mischievous to the true interests and proper sanctification of the Christian Sabbath.

The puritanic severity which restrains joyfulness and prohibits facilities for praise, and would shut up men on Sunday from the fresh air and the green fields, savors more of the Jewish rule of Death and Terror, than that of the merciful and loving Jesus, whose words, under the clear sky of Judea, should be the text words of all legal interpretations—"The Sabbath was made for man and not man for the Sabbath."

The Municipal Law recognizes man's need of a day of physical rest; its value in bringing new impulses to the industry of the country, by repairing its energies; its utility as promoting cleanliness, kind feelings and gentle manners; its valuable action on the intellect of the country, by its opportunities of instruction; and the aid that it gives to the law and order and stability of the social fabric, by sustaining in the public mind an enlightened and moral conscience. The Lord of the Sabbath, we may well believe, had regard to the same need in his enactment. Not the least of its benefits and blessings are those which belong to man in his social and personal relations—but his first duty is to God, and the institution of a Day consecrate to the worship, and service, and praise of the great Creator, fixes at once its duties. Rest from everything worldly and sinful: Action in everything heavenly and holy, should mark its sacred hours. You can not measure its value to you, as a Moral Being. You can not afford, as a good citizen, to lay by its salutary instructions and restraints.

And when you absent yourself from Church, or otherwise neglect the Duties of the Day, you not only lose, personally, those benefits and blessings with which it is fraught, but you do what in you lies, to cheer forward that Infidel Spirit, which would break down the barriers of law and order, and civilization and religion, and which hates the Lord's Day only because it hates every thing good.

This Day was "made for man." It was made for him, that he might learn who God is, and feel his obligations to such a Father. It was made for him that he might have time and space for Holy Worship: that he might see how guilty a prodigal he had lived, and go to his Father and say: "Father I have sinned against Heaven and before Thee; and am no more worthy to be called Thy son."

It was made for his observance, and not his idleness,[17] that he might cease from thoughts of business and worldliness; leave off customary employments, and be benefited by the effect of the abstinence upon his moral nature. It was made for him, that he might lift himself from Earth to Heaven, and prepare himself in Soul and Spirit for the field of his immortal Destiny. And in the solemn consecration of self to the duties of public and private religion, and to works of mercy and loving kindness, and the conscientious abstinence from secular employments, I look for the blessing of Almighty God upon the sanctification of the Lord's Day.

Brethren, I have said these words today, because I regard the invocation of legal restraint in behalf of religious duties to be of very questionable utility; and because a mistaken view of Sunday, in the light of Jewish observance, leads to such Pharisaic strictness of requirement, as tends to defeat its proper ends, and in nowise to commend it to the attention of those who practically disregard it. For yourselves, I feel sure you will give it the example of an enlightened sanctification. Prove your sense of its value, by its just and careful observance. Rejoice in it, as the day on which the Lord of Glory sealed his mission to the earth in the resurrection from the dead.[18] Teach your childreu to love its sacred hours, by making it for them a bright and happy day. Enjoy, thankfully, on that day, the good creatures of God He has given us; and remember, as the law of its observance, that "the Sabbath was made for man-and not man for the Sabbath," and that "the Son of Man is Lord, also, of the Sabbath Day."

1. "As there is no obligation to keep our Sabbath upon the same day as the Jews, so neither are we tied to their strict and rigorous manner of observing it. Our blessed Savior gives us the true notion of our duty, when he tells us, "the Sabbath was made for man, and not man for the Sabbath."—*Stackhouse's Bod. Div.*, p. 395.
2. "To-morrow is the rest of the Holy Sabbath unto the Lord." —Exodus 16:23.
3. "The same day being the first day of the week, when the disciples were assembled, came Jesus and stood in the midst."—20 John, 19.

    "Upon the first day of the week, let every one of you lay by him in store" — religious Offerings."—1 Cor. 16:2.

    "We should honor the day of the Resurrection, as the most excellent of days." —*St. Ignatius*, A. D. 116.

    "We joyfully celebrate the eighth day in memory of the Resurrection." —*St. Barnabas in the Apostolic Age.*

    "I, John, was in the spirit on the Lord's day."—Rev. 1:10.
4. "All persons within this Church, shall celebrate and keep the Lord's day, commonly called Sunday, in hearing the Word of God read and taught, in public and private prayer, in other exercises of devotion, and in acts of charity, using all godly and sober conversation."—39 *Can. of* 1808.

    "A table of Feasts to be observed in the Church throughout the year. All Sundays in the year."—*Book of Common Prayer.*
5. The Moral Duty is the observance of a Sabbath: the Positive Precept is the observance of the seventh day, or of the Sunday. If no moral duty were involved, in the law of the day, as enacted on Mount Sinai, then that law would become (what it is not,) a mere police regulation.

    There are some curious provisions of the Saxon Canons on this subject, which illustrate the simplicity of the times, and the purity of the early English Church, before the Bishop of Rome had jurisdiction there, which was not until the Norman conquest.

    A. D., 696. By King Wihtred's Laws, work was forbidden on Saturday night, as the preparation for the Lord's day.

    A. D. 747. By the 14th Canon of Cuthbert, Archbishop Canterbury, it was required that there shall be preaching on Sunday, as well as prayer.

    A. D. 957. The 23 Canon of Elfric enacts that the sense of the Gospel, the Lord's Prayer and the Creed, shall be explained to the people on Sundays, in English; 'for we ought to work and preach to laymen, lest they be lost in ignorance."

    A. D. 962. The 5th Canon of King Edgar, fixes the "holy time" of the Lord's day, from Saturday at 3 P. M., to Monday morning; and his 26th Canon requires the minister to keep the Church clean and in order, and to keep out the dogs and the pigs.

A. D. 994. The 7th and 8th of Theodulph's Capitula forbids corn and hay to be kept in the churches—forbids prayers to be said unless there be somebody to respond: and requires that Sunday be kept holy in all its hours.

6. "Let no man therefore, judge you in meat, or in drink, or in respect of an holy day, or of the new moon, or of the Sabbath-days; which are a shadow of things to come, but the body is of Christ.—2 Col. 16, 17.

The Apostle here speaks of the Jewish Sabbaths as having passed away; he classes them with matters which all agree are unimportant; he pronounces them "shadows:"—types of the body which is of Christ.

7. "And when the day of Pentecost was fully come, they were all with one accord in one place, and suddenly they were all filled with the Holy Ghost."—Acts 2:1, 2, 3.

8. "And God rested (or ceased) on the seventh day, from all his work which he had made, and God blessed the seventh day, (or portion,) and sanctified it, because (or since) that in it he had rested from all his work which God created and made."—Gen. 2:2, 3.

If God rested on the seventh day for the sake of the example, upon whom was the example intended to operate?—upon Jews or men in general? There is great significance, too, in the fact, that the only command in the Decalogue, which begins with the word "Remember," is that of the Resting-day or Sabbath.

9. St. Ignatius, A. D., 116, in his Epistle to the Magnesians, exhorts them to lay aside the observance of the Sabbath, and keep the Lords' day for a Festival, "wherein our life arose with Christ;" and Justin Martyr, next after him, tells us, that on Sundays, the Christians assembled out of all cities and villages for Divine service.

10. "It is no part of the object of the act to enforce the observance of a religious duty. The act does not, to any extent, rest upon the ground. that it is immoral or irreligious to labor on the Sabbath, any more than upon any other day. It simply prescribes a day of rest from motives of public policy, and as a wise regulation; and as the prohibition itself, is founded on principles of policy, upon the same principles certain exceptions are made, among which are works of necessity and charity." ..... "The necessity spoken of in the Statute, is not an absolute uncontrollable necessity only, but may be a necessity created by the exigencies of society or trade. If nothing but absolute necessity was intended, it would, in general, be unlawful to prepare a meal on the Sabbath; it would be equally unlawful to supply us with gas-light, for we might use candles previously laid in, or retire to beds at twilight, and so many things by all men admitted to be lawful, would be brought within the prohibition of the Statute."—*Thurman, C. J., in a very able opinion in McGatrick vs. Wason, 4 Ohio State Rept., 571.*

11. Exodus 16:29.
12. Exodus 35:3.
13. John 5:17.
14. Psalm 145:6.
15. Col. 2:15.
16. See McGatrick vs. Wason, 4 O. S. Rep., 567.
17. "It is our duty on Sunday to rise as early to the service of God, as we were wont on other days, to our worldly employment: to betake ourselves in secret, to the

supplication of Divine aid and benediction, to raise our affections to a suitable degree of love and reverence, by reading and meditation; to allow as little time as may be, to other necessary and convenient pursuits, until we repair from our closets to the Church. ... When the public worship is done, and we are returned from the solemn assembly, we must not think ourselves discharged from any other duty. Our children and servants, then, require our care to be instructed and encouraged each in his several capacity. When this is done, we may spend the rest of the day in religious and charitable offices, in a loving and christian communion one with another, in a thankful enjoyment of the good creatures of God: and fully shut up the whole day with prayer and thanksgiving, imploring forgiveness for the failings of the day, and asking that our imperfect services my be accepted through Jesus Christ our Lord."—Dr. Stackhouse, B. D., 397.

18. "The first day of the week cometh Mary Magdalene early while it was yet dark, unto the sepulchre, and seeth the stone taken away from the sepulchre." — John 20:1.

# PART II

# THE OFFICE OF MUSIC IN THE CHURCH OF GOD.

## A SERMON DELIVERED IN ST. PAUL'S CHURCH, CINCINNATI, ON THE FIFTH SUNDAY AFTER TRINITY, 1856.

"I will sing unto the Lord as long as I live: I will sing praise to my God while I have my being."

— PSALM 103:33

*To the Congregation of St. Paul's Church, this sermon preached at the reopening of their church organ, is affectionately inscribed, by their friend and pastor, P.H. Greenleaf.*

"Therefore with Angels and Archangels, and with all the company of Heaven, we laud and magnify thy glorious name; evermore praising Thee, and saying, Holy, holy, holy, Lord God of Hosts, Heaven and earth are full of thy glory. Glory be to Thee, O Lord Most High. Amen."

— COMMUNION OFFICE.

# SERMON

"Praise God in his Sanctuary: praise him with stringed instruments and organs. Let everything that hath breath praise the Lord."

— PSALM 150: 1, 4, 6.

THE praise and worship of God is the noblest employment of man. In his bodily organization, and in many of the attributes of his mind, he is the companion and sharer with other creatures. A bird of the air will rival him in the exercise of his memory, and a beast of the earth will surpass him in the tenacity of his affections. But when, in the consciousness of deep faith, and filled with strong sense of the gratitude he owes to God, man stands with face uplifted[1] to recognize, and worship and praise his great Creator—he towers above all earthly existence, and claims kindred with that Creator, as made in the "Image of God."[2]

It is the dignity of the employment, that elevates the praise of God, into the first rank of devotional exercises. The Church recognizes this as a chief object of the Lord's day service: for she declares we meet first of all "to set forth his most worthy praise." Praising God with the aid of "stringed instruments," and "organs," and all "the breath" of man, has from the beginning been accounted worthy our highest powers, and deserving the exercise of our best affections; and it is because of its dignity and importance that an inquiry into the most effective mode of engaging in it becomes pertinent and useful. Our subject, therefore, this morning, is the OFFICE OF MUSIC IN THE PRAISE OF GOD.

The praise of God demands the intelligent exercise of our highest intellectual powers, moved by the will and the affections. It is true that small intellects and feeble perceptions may praise God aright, and with strong will and deep affections; and no doubt the incense sent up from the fragrant bosom of the earth, in the morning sunlight, and the sounds spread abroad on the air by the sinless birds, and the murmurings of the brooks, and the rush of the river, and the diapasons of the sea, are all acceptable to the great Master of Life. But it is the nobility of man to bring to the altar of God the highest mental endowment, and employ the most transcendent intellectual powers in the adoration of their author. And we place, therefore, in the foreground of our subject, this thought: — that valuable praise and acceptable worship of God belong to the soul. and can never be brought to the test of any outward standard. It may be had most efficiently of all in churches, whose columns are living trees, and whose dome is the blue vault of Heaven; and it is best accomplished and expressed where there is the highest appreciation of the Divine nature, and the duty of man, and the fullest expression of the soul's uttermost feeling and affection.

In the impression and expression of those emotions, which belong to the praise of God, no means have been found, by human experience, so successful as musical sound. The principles of harmony seem to have been interwoven by God with the great elements of nature. They are heard in the song of the bird, the hum of the insect, and even from the very winds of heaven. The storm has its chords, and the river glides on in the cadence of musical numbers; while man himself is only a musical instrument of God's own making. These harmonial principles are perceived in him before he can utter articulate sounds. There are common chords in his bosom which thrill to the touch of feeling: which act and answer responsively; which make him capable of uttering by the voice, distinguishing by the ear, and feeling by the telegraphic nerves, every variety of sound. These chords speak to his soul. In the form of eloquence they enforce argument, give power to illustration, and sometimes control the judgment. They are adapted to receive and produce impression. You cannot hear the wail of pain or grief, but there is, in your heart, an echo of sadness. You cannot hear the glad ringing tones of childhood's joy, but there comes an echo of gladness. It is because your nervous organization was adapted by God to move the soul by the power of musical sounds, that we know it was designed so to be employed. And we maintain that this power of creating musical sounds—*i.e.*, language in tones—is capable of a religious use: that it is a mean of grace: that as a mean it has a two-fold office[3]—one to impress feeling, and another to express feeling; and that its highest, its legitimate and proper employment is the praise and glory of God.

To state these propositions is, in some sense, to prove them. The impression of their truth is so wide-spread, and the evidence of it so palpable and clear, that it is sufficient for our present purpose if we draw your attention to them as the basis of our views in the matter. They are the received and authorized judgments of the Church; and to them (so far as I know) the great body of Christians consent; so that we may assume, as our leading principle, that Music is a mean of grace.

What, then, is the office and place of a mean of grace but as a servant to serve? It is a mean to an end. It is valuable only so far as it conduces to the end. In itself and by itself, and disconnected from the end, it is out of place and without value: nay more, in relation to devotional sentiment, it may become an injury; and hence the importance of correct views as to its right use and office in the Church of God.

It will assist our judgment on this subject, if we first consider what place it had in the ancient Church; because I conceive it a safe ground of action to assume, that whatever principle was embodied in the ancient worship, and approved by God himself, still subsists as a guide to us, unless it can be shown that the reason for its institution has passed away.

Music, in the Jewish worship, was both vocal and instrumental; and was used as a medium of exciting emotion and feeling, and as a mode of expressing it when excited.

When the Prophet Elisha was inquired of by the King of Israel as to the divine will, he required a minstrel to play before him, to fit and prepare his mind for divine impression; and "it came to pass when the minstrel played, that the hand of Lord came upon him."[4]

So also we read that the Spirit of the Lord, departed from Saul, and an evil spirit from the Lord troubled him; and "it came to pass, when the evil spirit was upon him, that David took an harp and played with his hand, and the evil spirit departed from him."[5]

In the Temple service, the voices of the Levites and people were used in the praise of God, by the words of the hymns and songs of Moses, David, and others, assisted by instrumental music. And in the music there were more or less used eight different instruments: the Organ, which was only a set of Pandean pipes; the Tabret, resembling our tambourine; the Cymbals, like our cymbals in choruses; the Systrum, an iron bar, shaped like a tuning fork; the Dulcimer, a wind instrument of reeds; the Psaltery, called in 144 Psalm, "an instrument of ten strings;" the Harp; and the Trumpet. And at the dedication of the Temple "it came to pass, as the trumpeters and singers were as one to make one sound to be heard in praising and thanking the Lord; and when they lifted up their voice, with trumpets, and cymbals, and instruments of music, and praised the Lord, saying, He is good, for his mercy endureth forever, that *then* the house was filled with a cloud, even the house of the Lord, so that the priests could not stand to minister, for the glory of the Lord had filled the house of God."[6]

Here we have record of God's blessing and approbation of the choral singing of prepared forms of praise, assisted by trumpets and instruments. It is a blessing upon Congregational chanting of Psalms of David, assisted by the organ, with the trumpet stop open. It is the Divine approbation, (so far as it is anything,) of vocal music, used to express devotional feeling, and assisted and subserved by instrumental tones.

Indeed the Psalms of David were expressly written to be *sung* and not read; and the recent action of the Presbyterian General Assembly,[7] and other religious bodies, approving the chanting of the Psalms, instead of singing them in metre,[8] shows that Christian sentiment is returning to the "old paths and good ways" of our fathers. Even we ourselves would approach nearer to the Divine pattern if the Psalter for the day was always *chanted or sung* instead of being read, as is here accustomed. The invitation in the Venite of our morning service, is "O come let us *sing* [not read] unto the Lord." And I hope the day is not distant when every morning's sunlight will witness the daily praise of the Lord in this his Sanctuary, by Psalms of David, with instruments and organ tones and the breath he has given us.

So far, then, as analogies go, the Jewish practice gives us the key to the right use of musical sounds in the house of God. They are there as servants and not masters. As servants they are to serve and be subservient. As servants they are to obey the proprieties and regard the character of the place where they are used. As servants they are not principal figures and chief objects. They wait. They attend. They do bidding. They carry and convey. And there their office ceases. They are used, but only to promote the ends and objects of the assembly. If they inspire or elevate devotional sentiment; if they stimulate the coldness of the sluggish heart; if they tend to melt its selfishness, to refine its sensibilities, to prepare it for holy influences, and above all, if they enable it to give expression to its deeply-seated feeling, they have fulfilled their office. Their place in the Jewish service is their place in the Christian service—to serve, and not to govern and rule. And Pliny's report to the Emperor

Trajan, that the Christians of his time met together in a worship which he characterizes, as a vocal chanting, responsively, of prepared hymns to Christ,[9] recognizes the principle that musical sounds are to serve devotional sentiment; and that any other place for them, whether vocal or instrumental, is contrary to their design and use, under the Jewish and primitive Christian dispensations.

It follows, then, that all musical sounds in public worship must have a character in accordance with the reverence due to the place, and the object of the assembly. They must not be "light and unseemly,"[10] "indecorous or profane." Their character must be grave, dignified, solemn; calculated to convey, by their tones, devout feeling, and to act effectively in promoting the grand design of all that takes place in Christian assemblies and Christian Churches. Since, then, singing is only "melodious saying," and music is only "language in tones," it must be obvious that simplicity of melody and harmony should be a leading principle in the selection; that regard should be had to the greatest good of the greatest number; and that in order to subserve the purposes of the assembly, that impression should be made which will best suit those purposes; and that expression should be afforded. which will best utter and convey the cries of a soul to its God.

Observe the music of the ancient Church; how simple, how expressive, how dignified, how grave![11] It has a character of its own; and you can never hear a true Gregorian chant without an impression of the sanctity of its tones. See, too, in the primitive worship, that the harmonies are syllabic, designed not for versification, but the dignity and gravity of prose; that they are intended for the multitude, and therefore divided so that the multitude can sing.

Come down to later days. Listen to the good Archbishop Cranmer: "The song that shall be made thereto, [i. e., to the Psalter] should not be full of notes; but as near as may be, for every syllable a note, so that it may be sung distinctly and devoutly." Nor was the Queen Elizabeth less direct and plain in her commands: "The Queen willeth that there be a modest and distinct song used in all parts of the Common Prayer in the Church, that the same may be understood of the people, as if it were read without singing."[12]

Here was the true principle developed: "Understanded of the people, as if it were read without singing," lies at the foundation of all true use of musical sounds in expression of praise. From A. D. 1557, when only eight tunes were "allowed to be sung in Churches," down to modern times, this has been the idea upon which musical directions have been issued. And even the rich contributions to English Church Music made by Handel, Beethoven, Tallis, Croft, the Burneys, and others, have been chiefly distinguished for simple melody, generally syllabic, highly expressive of sentiment, and so plain as to engage the attention and affections of the people. Applying, therefore, to worshiping assemblies this principle, devotional sentiment, (or which is here the same thing, the praise of God), is best expressed by simple melodies, common to all, employed by all, and capable of such distinct and clear utterance and enunciation as can be "understanded of the people." I can conceive no good reason why the music or tunes of the Church Service should not be as fixed as the words; so that on the recurrence of an Anthem or hymn, the words should suggest the music, and the music, the words; save only that such regard should be had to the season as that the major or minor key should be used. Our devotions are always hindered by novelties. New music is objectionable, simply because it is new; and the idea of frequent change to prevent weariness, will only apply where lack of devotional feeling is sought to be supplied by musical sentiment. The object to be attained is praise. That which will unite the greatest number[13] in such praise is generally the best mean. And I appeal to your experience, if your own prayers and praises are not best expressed in words and tunes to which you have been accustomed. In a word, Congregational singing,[14] or the chanting of Anthems and other suitable words in musical sounds, whose character is Church-like, dignified, reverential, and in harmony with the great realities which are subjects of the praise of God—this is the true method of expressing praise.

It follows from this, that two classes of tones or sounds must be excluded from Church. 1st. Those which, from any general law of association, recall persons, places, or things at war with devotional sentiment. 2d. Those which, having been born and cradled in the voluptuous atmosphere of the opera and ball-room, have a character and leave an impress which are not favorable to the dignity and sanctity of the Service. You can all bear testimony to the mischiefs, which have sometimes resulted from the use of these two classes of sounds; and no other argument against them is necessary than to appeal to experience.

For similar reasons, I would recommend the use of prose rather than verse to express devotional feelings. The use of rhyme in worship is a modern invention, wholly unknown to the ancient Church. The expression of religious feeling through such instrumentality is not always effective, often imperfect, and in many respects unworthy the dignity and character of the subject.

There are, no doubt, some highly devotional sentiments suitably expressed in verse in our Psalms and Hymns; but they are expressed, I think, with more dignity and propriety in prose;[15] and as no attempt to translate the Psalms of David into English verse has been successful, I may ask you to test the matter by comparing the 124th Selection in metre, which you sang this morning, with the majestic simplicity of the same Psalm in the Psalter. The truth is, that Metrical Psalmody began during the great Reformation from Popery, and the songs of the reformers swept over Europe, with the popular Protestant tornado, much as the songs of the political campaign of 1840 swept over the Union. But their exciting character, and the very metrical dress, which so deeply moved the popular mind, render them less suited to the staid gravity and dignified simplicity of the public worship; and I think experience has proved that a text of Scripture, or words of solemn prayer or praise, are expressed better in the plain majesty of prose, than in the jingle of rhyme.

You will at once see that these same principles apply to the tones of instrumental music. Their office is to serve, to give expression to the soul's feeling, and to convey impression to the devotional thought; and nothing is better suited to both than the tones of a Church Organ.[16] If its pipes could speak, there is not a text of Scripture which it would not utter with dignity and reverence; and hence, from its peculiar conformation, its great value in the Church service. But it is only a servant, and should be kept only to serve. Its voluntaries and interludes, its chords and tones, should all be directed to the great ends and objects of the public assembly. "Holiness to the Lord," should be emblazoned above the key-board; and as a director of public impression, it should be held strictly to the laws of its being, as a servant, and not a master.

Indeed, our entire Ritual service is constructed upon the principle that the people, (not the minister or organist only), are the worshipers; that the people have words and tones supplied for their use; and that unless the people bear their part and occupy their place in the public service, that service is mutilate and incomplete. The value of words and tones in public worship lies neither in their intrinsic beauty, their grammatical accuracy, nor the excellence of their construction; but in their fitness to impress the popular mind with the true nature, dignity and character of the place and the assembly, and their adaptation to express suitably those ascensions of soul, those deeply seated feelings of prayer and praise to Almighty God, which are alone deserving the name of public worship.

These are my views upon this great subject. I think they accord with the true character of our Ritual service. I have not descended into details of modes and ways, because that rather belongs to "persons skilled in music," and to other times and places. I have only stated principles, from which duties result; and I leave them to your own application.

In all the Anthems of the Church Service, from the grand Te Deum of St. Ambrose to the "Gloria,"[17] which precedes the Gospel for the day, esteem it a privilege to bear your appropriate part.

Consider your voices as given you by God, for the very purpose of expressing your wants, and conveying your praise. One of the Fathers of the early Church wrote, fifteen centuries ago, that the "Amen" of the Church Service of his time was like a clap of thunder. Oh, how impressive our own beautiful Ritual would be if such thunders were heard among us! Esteem it a delight to use your voice in its Maker's praise.[18] Let strangers to our mode of worship see and feel, from the manly response and the vocal chords of the whole congregation, that this is a Church *for the people*; that this is a worshiping assembly. It is true, words and sounds do not constitute prayer or praise; they are only servants. But they are kept here to serve, and to serve you. They are meant to express the feelings of your soul; and when you read of the employments of Heaven, that there was heard "the voice of a great multitude, as the voice of many waters, and as the voice of mighty thunderings, saying, Alleluia, for the Lord God omnipotent reigneth," be glad to imitate these celestial harmonies. Be glad to begin here on earth to join your voice to the multitude, as a member of that kingdom in which the Lord God omnipotent reigneth! "Praise God in His sanctuary; praise Him with stringed instruments and organs; let every thing that hath breath praise the Lord."

---

1. "Os hominis sublime dedit cœlum tueri, jussit et erectos ad sidera tollere vultus."
2. Genesis 1:27.
3. "In harmony the very image and character even of virtue and vice is perceived, the mind delighted with their resemblances, and brought, by having them often iterated, into a love of the things themselves. For which cause there is nothing more contagious and pestilent than certain kinds of harmony-than some nothing more strong and potent unto good. And that there is such a difference of one kind from another, we need no proof but our own experience, inasmuch as we are at the hearing of some more inclined unto sorrow and heaviness; of some more mollified and softened in mind; one kind apter to stay and settle us, another to move and stir our affections; there is that draweth to a marvellous grave and sober mediocrity; there is also that carrieth, as it were into ecstacies, filling the mind with an heavenly joy, and for the time in a manner severing it from the body... The prophet David having, therefore, singular knowledge, not in poetry alone, but in music also, judged them both to be things most necessary

for the house of God, left behind him to that purpose, a number of divinely indited poems, and was further the author of adding unto poetry melody in public prayer—melody both vocal and instrumental, for the raising up of men's hearts, and the sweetening of their affections toward God. In which consideration, the Church of Christ doth likewise at this present day retain it as an ornament to God's service, and an help to our own devotion".—*Hooker, Book* v, 515.
4. 2 Kings 3:15.
5. 1 Samuel 16:23.
6. 2 Chronicles 5:13.
7. The New School Presbyterian Assembly lately had up the subject of singing the Psalter before it, and the following are two of the resolutions adopted by the Committee on Psalmody:
    That a Committee be appointed to prepare a selection of the Psalms of David, in a separate book, for Congregational singing and chanting.
    That the said Committee be directed to prepare as speedily as possible an arrangement of the entire Book of Psalms upon the plan proposed, and report to a future General Assembly.
8. "Whenever the Hymns are used in the celebration of divine service, a certain portion of the Psalms of David, in metre, shall also be sung." This direction, found in our Prayer-books at the end of the Hymns, never was an enactment by any authority; and is not so understood. Indeed, unless both Psalms and Hymns were sung together, at the same time, a literal compliance would be impossible.
9. "Carmenque Christo, quasi Deo, dicere secum invicem."—Epist. lib x. Ep. 97.
10. "It shall be the duty of every Minister, with such assistance as he can obtain from persons skilled in music, to give order concerning the tunes to be sung at any time in his Church; and especially it shall be his duty to suppress all light and unseemly music, and all indecency and irreverence in the performance, by which vain and ungodly persons profane the service of the sanctuary."—*Prayer Book.*
11. The most ancient form of Church music is chanting. This was the sacred music of the Hebrews. Their language did not admit of metre, in the modern sense of the word. Their poetry, so far as outward structure was concerned, consisted in a certain measured and balanced construction of sentences, such as we find in the Book of Psalms. Rhyming metres, indeed, were unknown to all the ancients. In the middle ages, many hymns were composed in rhyme in the Latin language, some of which, though barbarous compositions according to the classical standard, are very exquisite specimens of devotional poetry. One of them, the Dies Iræ, is known to us in a very free translation of Sir Walter Scott's, "The day of wrath, that dreadful day." Chanting came early into use among Christians, and was undoubtedly in use among them from "the beginning of the Gospel," and is the singing spoken of in the New Testament. The early chanting was plain, simple and severe; was indeed little more than reading with an intonation, and a slight variation of musical notes at the close. The Gregorgian chants, so called from one of the popes by whom the music of the Church was reformed and reduced to a system, are of this description in its more polished state.

In modern times, the chant has become more ornate and complicated, and been allowed to admit a greater variety of notes and changes; and whether single or double, that is, consisting of a single strain constantly repeated; or of two related strains following one another alternately, is susceptible of a considerable degree of variety and compass.

Chanting is a favorite species of music in the Church, and whether in its simple or more complex varieties, is well adapted to delight the ear and promote the spirit of devotion.—*Hallam on Morning Prayer*, 98.

12. Injunctions to the Clergy, 49.
13. I recommemd the congregational singing of the air or tune in unison, the parts to be supplied by the Choir and Organ. This is the practice of the Lutheran Churches, and produces a fine effect.
14. The following excellent counsels of Bishop McIlvaine to his Clergy, though familiar to you, I repeat, as commending them to your thoughtful attention:

    "CONGREGATIONAL SINGING, with or without the aid of an organ and a choir, is the only singing that answers the ends of public worship. The performance of music by a choir often seems to be considered the whole attainment to be desired, as if to listen to performances, instead if to worship with voice and heart, were the whole duty of man, in that part of our services. But can we consent to this? Where is the remedy? Do you say the people will not sing? Certainly they will not, when chants and tunes are sung that are so new, so difficult, so often changed for others equally new, that not only have they never learned them, but learn them they can not. But how is it when so familiar a tune as Old Hundred is sung? Do not the people then unite? Why? Because tunes are sung which are familiar—so simple as to be easily learned—so adapted that no special cultivation of ear or voice is needed for their adoption. And if you would see to it that such tunes and chants alone are sung; if you will prevent this constant introduction of new music, without the least regard to the rights of the congregation; if you will see to it that, not display of voices, nor exhibition of art, but simply the devotional feelings and profit of the people, are consulted in the selection of the chants and tunes, and in the manner of their execution, you will remove all the causes that have led to the evils we now deplore, and will do very much to elevate our public worship, in this very important branch, to a measure of interest in which, in some places of worship, where there are neither choirs nor organs, we are far exceeded, in the judgment of the truly spiritual worshiper."

15. Compare, also, the 7th Hymn with the 19th Psalm, in the Psalter; the 9th Hymn with 23d Psalm; 61st Hymn with 63d chapter of Isaiah; the 2d verse of the 144th Hymn with the 10th verse of 41 Isaiah; the 154th Hymn with the 100th Psalm; the 159th Hymn with the 42d Psalm; the 188th Hymn with the 14th chapter of the book of Job; the 106th Hymn with the 35th Isaiah, 2d verse, and others. What is the 134th Hymn, when sung, (with the exception of its beautiful close), but a singing of definitions.
16. We find organs in the Church as early as the seventh century, 1200 years ago, and here let all the admirers of the musical art stop awhile to reflect with gratitude and devotion that the invention of choral harmony in parts arose from the Trinitarian worship of the Christian Church. —*See Jones of Nayland's Sermons*, pp. 574. 578.

17. This custom of giving glory to God for his holy Gospel, appears to have prevailed from remote antiquity in all the Churches of the East and the West; and by custom, the rubric inserted in the American Common Prayer-book, from the first book of Edward VI, requiring it to be said, has been interpreted to mean a saying in musical cadence. The expressive Gloria, in our use, was arranged by Weiss from an ancient German Chant.— *See Palmer's Origines Liturgica*, 2d *Vol.*, 51.
18. The Te Deum in our use is by Meineke; the Gloria in Excelsis is No. 2 Wainwright; the Venite, the Jubilate, the Benedictus, and other Chants, with the usual Gloria Patris, are all sung in Gregorian tones.

# PART III

# THE SUBSTANCE OF A SERMON

DELIVERED IN SAINT JOHN'S CHURCH, CHARLESTOWN, (MASS.), FEBRUARY 19, 1843.

# SERMON

*"Here have we no continuing city."*

— HEBREWS 13:14.

A "CONTINUING CITY," a secure condition, a home on the earth, is the natural desire of man. The young voyager in life, as he casts forward his anticipations to the future, is nerved to face "the battle and the breeze," that he may secure a permanent abode; that he may play well his part; that he may have shelter from the coming storms of life; and, at the last, repose, in domestic happiness, like the bird, with those that nestle in his bosom. As time and Providence befall, the desire increases. The way of life is overcast, the path is rough and thorny, and that desire which in youth was but an aspiration, becomes the absorbing feeling of advancing years. Every disappointed hope renews its strength. Every calamity that occurs, every infirmity that grows upon him, increases the longing of the heart for that place of permanent security, beautifully imaged by the apostle as a "continuing city."

Observe the imagery. A land is swept by desolating enemies.

Trial, trouble, and sorrow, beset the way; "temptation without," and "corruption within." The coast is unprotected; the lines of empire unguarded; armed foes carry plunder and ruin over the face of the earth. But "the fortified city" is a "refuge" from all. Crowned with bastioned walls, planted on a rock, armed and fortified to resist every aggression, what could be more desirable to the hunted and the oppressed? And this desirable refuge, this permanent home, is called "a continuing city." Now, upon every object and desire belonging to this lower world, upon every fabric of hope, and castle of happiness, founded upon the earth, God hath written, "it abideth not." In the wise and merciful government of our heavenly Father, it seems to be ordered, that the very circumstances of our existence here, —our pains, our imperfections, our disappointments, and our griefs, should stand up, tangible and sensible memorials, along the pathway of our pilgrimage, pointing our hopes toward heaven, and admonishing us, that we should seek something more secure and certain than can be found in a changing and faithless world. Here, but as pilgrims, our residences and employments are only a succession of temporary encampments. Today, the plan is laid, the hope entertained, and the fabric builded; the tent is pitched, its canvas whitens in the air, and tomorrow, it is borne to another and a distant spot, to be again pitched, and struck, and moved, until it is seen no more forever. And the apostle of God presents us, in this land of vanishing shadows, the hopes of the gospel, as the only realities of our pilgrim condition, and bids us seek the better home to come, because, as runs the admonition of our text, "Here, we have no continuing city."

And who does not need the admonition? How many, even today, are thinking of future earthly plans and expectations, for themselves and near and dear ones, only to be disappointed! How many are building castles of earthly hope, and spending energies and affections on earthly objects, only to see the fairest castle thrown down, and the dear object of love cut off, and, like a broken flower, left to wither and die. Nay, even when these expectations become realities, who does not know that half their glory has departed? Hope, like the Indian honey-bird, flits from object to object, perpetually in advance of us; the most successful man is never fully happy, never fully blest.

And when the earthly prize is gained, what is it? Wealth and luxury have poured their stores at your feet; happy faces and dear friends surround you; intellect, refinement, congenial taste, complete your circle of enjoyment. Nay, more; upon all these, Religion pours down a flood of perpetual sunshine, and your dwelling beams with the light of holiness; and yet upon this terrestrial paradise, God often writes, "it abideth not." You cannot shut out sin from this Eden; there is no Ithuriel-spear to touch the tempters of our race, and your city cannot and does not exclude trial, and trouble, and sorrow. The happiness you enjoy seems permanent, but the moment you connect it with the earth, it is, like the gathered flower which children plant, gay, fragrant, and beautiful, but it has neither root nor stalk; it must fade and wither in the grasp. Set your earthly city ever so high above the common accidents of life, set it so that its battlements seem firm, its warders vigilant, its towers pointing toward heaven, "as if partaking of its eternity," and yet how frail and glassy are the very first stones upon which its foundations rest, our lives. "We bring our years to an end as it were a tale that is told." It is heard and forgotten; its words sounded upon the ear, and vanished into empty air. "So soon passeth our life away and we are gone," like a tale that is told, like a forgotten story, like a vapor, says St. James, "that appeareth for a little time, and then vanisheth away." O, how often and how touchingly are we admonished of this! And never, my friends, more strongly than by the circumstances of our assembly this morning. When we last met in this holy place, it was surrounded by festival wreaths and joyous recollections; but O, what an admonition have we had, that all these earthly scenes are, from us, fast passing away!

A dear little child of the congregation, a lamb of Christ's flock, here, but yesterday, to sing her little hymn, and learn her little prayer at Jesus' feet, now sleeps in yonder grave!

[Henrietta Robinson, daughter of Hon. Frederick Robinson, President of the Senate, died Feb. 13, after an illness of a few hours, aged 6 years.]

And next, the young wife and mother, one so lately here, to receive at this altar the pledges of a Savior's dying love, — one, so faithful and affectionate as a wife, so truthful and gentle as a friend, — one, whose shining excellence and rare accomplishments were adorned by the "beauty of holiness," — she has departed this life, and we mourn the loss of so much that was Christian and excellent from our social circle.

[Mrs. Sarah Easton Ladd Taylor, wife of Rev. Fitch W. Taylor, chaplain U. S. Navy, died in Charlestown, February 12, and was interred in a vault in Trinity Church, Boston, on the morning of the day of Bishop Griswold's death.]

And then, to fill the cup of our bereavement, and add impression to the lesson, God hath taken our Father to himself! Our venerable friend and Bishop, the successor of an apostle in his office, the follower of Jesus in his life, the earthly head and governor of our Church, has gone to his rest. His pastoral staff is broken. The head which hath worn the miter, for more than thirty years, with so much dignity, and usefulness, and honor, —the hand which hath so long conveyed to able and faithful men the divine commission of the Christian ministry, —and the heart which so anxiously beat for the welfare and happiness of the Church, all are laid low in the dust; and, full of years and honors, our father has gone to his rest. He died, like a Christian warrior, on the field of action, with his armor girded, his spear in rest, in very act of duty, manfully warring, as a good soldier of Jesus Christ, against the world, and sin, and Satan; and the crown of life is his reward. He died, as he had lived, (as we all might hope and pray to live and die,) "in the communion of the catholic church, in the confidence of a certain faith, in the comfort of a reasonable, religious, and holy hope, at peace with God, in charity with man." And the little Child, and the faithful Woman, and the good old Man, are gathered and garnered in their rest; and we are here, before God, this morning, spared thus far by his forbearing mercy; and these tokens of woe which surround us, tell us, with a voice we cannot choose but hear, that " here have ye no continuing city."

["The reader will perceive that this sermon is chiefly devoted to the consideration of the character of Bishop Griswold; but, in consequence of the sudden death of Mrs. Fitch Taylor, during the same week that our venerable Bishop was called from us, the author could not refrain from an allusion to one, who was so much an ornament of her sex.]

Death is always solemn, always subduing, always impressive. In the humblest visitation we recognize the divine hand; yet, here the impression is confined to a narrow circle. Individual hopes are crushed; the happiness of a family is blasted, and deep is the sorrow buried in the bosom of the stricken. Yet the community sustains no visible injury; the vibration of domestic sorrow extends but little way, and lasts not long. The arrow of the Almighty hath glided through the air, to the bosom where he hath sent it, but the air has closed upon its track, and without, all is peaceful and serene. But when the great lights of a community, placed aloft for the guidance of inferior movements, are extinguished, then, most impressively does God speak. And such a bereavement is ours! Our spiritual father and guide has gone down to the grave, under circumstances of peculiar interest. More than thirty years ago, he was summoned to assume the dignity of the apostolic office. But alas, as in apostolic days, to minister to a scattered and dispersed flock. And faithfully did he execute it. In season, and out of season, through good report, and evil report, did he guide and govern the church of God, and fight the good fight of faith.

Admonished, by his many and often infirmities, the decay of bodily vigor and the flight of years, that here he could have no continuing city, he attempted, on several occasions, to procure an assistant in his office. His language to the Massachusetts Convention, in September last, was, "No one Bishop of our Church has, at my advanced age, ever attempted to do one half of the amount of Episcopal duties which are needed in the Eastern Diocese; and if any say I am doing much, let him consider with what wearisome labor I do it, and how very soon the time must come, when I can do it no longer." Arguments like these deeply impressed us. In the good providence of God, and by an unanimity, such as was never, on a like occasion, known in our country, our present bishop was elected, to assist him while living, and succeed him, when departed; and scarce three months have passed, since our late father, in this place where I now stand, congratulated us all on the happy result.

[Rt. Rev. Manton Eastburn, D. D., was elected to the Bishopric of Massachusetts, September 27, 1843, at the first ballot, by the unanimous voice of both orders; a circumstance without precedent in the history of the American branch of the Church Catholic.]

Here, in this place, he [Griswold] met the deputies from his several churches for the last time. Here, were uttered his last prayers for us. Here, he gave us his final benediction.

[The last Convention of the Eastern Diocese assembled in St John's Church, Charlestown. The Diocese is now dissolved.]

Scarce six weeks have passed, since the elected assistant was consecrated to his holy office. Scarce three days have gone by, since the good old Bishop himself, walked to the house of his successor, and, as if to deliver up to him the miter and the pastoral staff, the badges of his office, laid down in his presence, and died at his feet. How fitting, how singularly beautiful and appropriate, was that Providence, which thus prepared the way before him, and ordered thus the surrender of his holy office. And we are here, today, to testify our affection for our father, to deplore his loss, and to be taught by his example, as we long have been by his precepts.

HE HAS LEFT us *the example of his humility*. Himself, the chief Bishop of the Church in our land, this eminent prelate was distinguished, among us all, for his remarkable humility; —a grace, frowned upon by the world, derided by the philosophic infidel, but a gem resplendent in that crown of life that fadeth not away. It was not that he ostentatiously took the lowest place. No man had more just sense of the real dignity of his office. It was not that he habitually disparaged his own talents, or spoke of his own imperfections and faults. But he had acquired the rare art of forgetting himself. The grace of humility so shone in all that he said and did, nay, even played upon his countenance as we beheld him, as that he might literally be said to be "clothed with it." If it kept him reserved in his conversation, retiring in his habits of life, and, as it were, in a perpetual shade, aside from the great currents of the world, it gave him that dignity and simplicity of character which compelled involuntary homage from men, wherever he moved in society. Even those of us, who met him in the intimacies of his own fireside, familiarly, as our dear father and friend, could not fail to notice and respect that lovely forgetfulness of self, which marked his entire intercourse with us, official and personal. And he has gone to receive his reward, for "blessed are the poor in spirit for theirs is the kingdom of heaven." Let us follow him, as he followed Christ. Let self be forgotten in the strife to do good and love. "In lowness of mind let each esteem other better than themselves. Look not every man on his own things, but every man also on the things of others. Let this mind be in you which was also in Christ Jesus, who, being in the form of God, made himself of no reputation and took upon form the form of a servant."

HE HAS LEFT us *the example of gentleness and affection*. His was the temper that reviled not again; when "he suffered he threatened not, but committed himself to him that judgeth righteously." Even his anger was, like that spoken of by an ancient father, but as bubbles which bead the surface of pure water when agitated, and leave not a taint of sediment behind. He cherished no resentments. He remembered no injuries. And though, from the keenness of his sensibilities, and the delicacy of his feelings, he was peculiarly exposed to the wounds and injuries a tender mind will always receive from contact with the world, yet none was more ready to forbear and endure, and none quicker to forgive. Gentle, kind, and affectionate to all, careful of wounding the feelings of others, and tender of their fame, he was known only to be loved, and loved most by those who knew him best. Like that disciple, whom Jesus loved, and whose character was but the "counterfeit presentment" of his own, his exhortation continually to all, and especially to us, his sons in the ministry, was, "love one another." Such should ever be our character. A common faith, a common Lord, a common prayer, and drinking at the same fountain the same waters of life, — these are ties of no mean strength. Let us feel their force and cherish their influence. Animated, no less by the example of our venerated father than by his precepts, let us honor his memory by emulating his example.

He has left us the example of unaffected and habitual piety. A man of prayer, his life, like the clear unclouded sunshine of a summer's day, was resplendent in light from above. Literally, he walked with God. God was in all his thoughts. It has been my privilege, from early youth, to have been honored with the friendship, the counsel, and occasional society and correspondence of this great and good man; and truly, I know not the man who more habitually, and, as it were, instinctively, acknowledged God in all his ways. In his last letter to me, a brief note received but two days before his death, he notifies me of his intention to spend Sunday, the 5th of March next, with me, adding, with his accustomed humility and piety, 'if the Lord permit." And though that permission was withheld, and the Lord has taken to himself our venerable father, yet I desire to thank God that he has so long spared him to us, and that although he has departed, and the sun of his usefulness, in this life, has forever set, yet there fingers still in our sky, the sunset glory of his undying example. Brethren, let us follow him as he followed Christ. "Go to now, ye that say, today or tomorrow we will go into such a city, and continue there a year, and buy and sell, and get gain, whereas ye know not what shall be on the morrow; for that ye ought to say, if the Lord will, we shall do this, or that." Let us imitate our venerable father, and temper every hope and every prospect of the future, with that pious resignation which said, "If the Lord permit."

My friends, in his humility, in his gentleness, in his unaffected and habitual piety, our father yet lives. "Being dead he speaketh." And, in the light of his example, and by the impressive lessons he has taught, he would bid us go forth to daily duty, mindful that here we have not and cannot have a continuing city. There is a City, eminently a continuing city, whose builder and maker is God. It abideth forever. Its embattled walls can never be thrown down. Its holy foundations can never be disturbed. Its felicity is eternal. Into this city, no pain, no sorrow, no affliction or trial can come. "God shall wipe away all tears." And his own eternal promise and presence is security for the happiness and glory of its residence. Thither has our venerable father ascended; and while, in this bereavement, we are solemnly admonished, that here we have not, and cannot have for ourselves, or those near and dear to us, a continuing city, we are also bidden, to seek one to come, eternal in the heavens, a city God hath prepared for those who love and serve him.

# ALEXANDER VIETS GRISWOLD

THE RIGHT REV. ALEXANDER VIETS GRISWOLD was born, April 22, 1766, in Simsbury, in the State of Connecticut. The Bishop, speaking of himself, has said, "My case so far resembles that of Timothy, that my mother's name was Eunice, and my maternal grandmother, Lois; from both of whom, as he is in his case, I received much early instruction. By their teaching, from a child I have known the Holy Scriptures, which were able (had I rightly used the knowledge), to make me wise unto salvation. To the care of my mother, especially, instilling into my tender mind sentiments of piety, and the duty of prayer, and the knowledge of Christ, I was very much indebted. Though I have sinned much, and in everything come short of what should have been my improvement under such advantages, through the Lord's merciful goodness, the fear of God, and the love of his name and of the religion of Christ, have never been wholly lost. I had early experience of the comforts of a religious hope; how well founded, it is not now necessary to inquire. At the age of about ten years, I was reduced by distressing sickness to the verge of the grave, and for several hours was supposed to be dying. And I can never forget with what lively hope and joy unspeakable, amidst great bodily suffering, I looked forward to the blessedness of the heavenly state. Should it please the Lord at the time near at hand, when I shall be indeed at the point to die, to vouchsafe me the like peace and joy in believing, how could I worthily magnify his name! Had I then died, it would not, probably, by anyone now living, be remembered or known that such a person ever existed. So soon are we forgotten here; but the righteous shall be had in everlasting remembrance. Whether it would have been better for me to have died then, God only knows. He had, it seems, a work for me to do."

The Bishop has further remarked, when alluding to his early history, "There was one circumstance of my life which I would ever think and speak of with thankfulness. About the time of my birth, the Rev. Roger Viets, my mother's brother, returned from England, in priest's orders, and took charge of the parish in which I lived. For several years he resided in my father's family; and the most of my time, till my twentieth year, I lived with him. He was a thorough scholar, and excelled in the talent of communicating knowledge to others. From my childhood, he had a strong partiality and fondness for me, and was at great pains to instruct me in everything which he supposed might be useful to me in this life, and especially in classical knowledge. Even when *laboring in the field*, (for in those days country clergymen thought it no disgrace or departure from duty to labor, as St. Paul did, for temporal things,) which hundreds of days we did together, he would still continue his instructions."

At the age of twenty, he was confirmed by Bishop Seabury, and became a communicant; and was married at about the same period. In June 1795, being then twenty-nine years of age, he received deacon's orders, and in October of the same year, he was ordained priest. His first parochial charge consisted of the parishes of

Plymouth, Harwington and Litchfield, in Connecticut. In 1804, he became the Rector of St. Michael's Church, Bristol, R.I. It was while rector of this church, he was called to the Episcopate of the Eastern Diocese, and was consecrated in Trinity Church, New York, May 29, 1811, by Bishop White, Bishops Provost and Jarvis being present and assisting.

During his Episcopate, he ordained 171 deacons, and 128 priests, and confirmed 12,104 persons. The States originally composing his diocese, contained, at the time of his election, 15 clergymen. At his death, the same States numbered 116 clergymen. He died the 15th of February 1843, in the 77th year of his age, and on the 31st of his Episcopate.

# ABOUT THE AUTHOR

Patrick Henry Greenleaf (1807-1869), born in Maine, was the son of famed American lawyer and jurist Simon Greenleaf (1783-1853). He was a graduate of Bowdoin College, where he was a classmate of Henry Wadsworth Longfellow and Nathaniel Hawthorne and other $19^{th}$ century luminaries, and after college became a practicing lawyer for a few years, before training for the ministry. He pursued theological studies under the Episcopalian Bishop George Washington Doane (1799-1859) and was ordained a deacon by Bishop Alexander V. Griswold (1766-1843). For several years Greenleaf was the Rector of St. John's Church, Charlestown, Mass.; also of St. Paul's Church, Cincinnati, Ohio, and in 1862 became Rector of Emmanuel Church in Brooklyn, New York, where he died at the age of 62, on June 21, 1869.

www.ingramcontent.com/pod-product-compliance
Lightning Source LLC
Chambersburg PA
CBHW052127070526
44586CB00016B/2112